REDBACK publishing

DROUGHT IN AUSTRALIA

BY JOHN LESLEY

First Published 2024 by
Redback Publishing
Suite 6, 13a Narabang Way,
Belrose NSW 2085
Australia

www.redbackpublishing.com
info@redbackpublishing.com

ISBN 978-1-922322-91-3

Author: John Lesley
Editor: Caroline Thomas
Designer: Redback Publishing

Original illustrations © Redback Publishing 2024
Originated by Redback Publishing

Acknowledgements
Abbreviations: l—left, r—right, b—bottom, t—top, c—centre, m—middle
We would like to thank the following for permission to reproduce photographs: (Images © shutterstock)
P7t Postmodern Studio / Shutterstock.com, p7b © Commonwealth of Australia 2021, Bureau of Meteorology. - IDCK200A00, p13tr Edward Haylan / Shutterstock.com, p14bl Alex Cimbal / Shutterstock.com, p15l Nils Versemann / Shutterstock.com, p15r Alex Cimbal / Shutterstock.com, p17t Anna LoFi / Shutterstock.com, p21t State Library of South Australia, PRG 1258/1/3014, p21m awm-media, p21b State Library of New South Wales, p22t/m/b awm-media, p23l Museums Victoria, p23r State Library of Victoria, p25br Anna LoFi / Shutterstock.com, p28bl My_Aussie_Adventures / Shutterstock.com

NATIONAL LIBRARY OF AUSTRALIA

A catalogue record for this book is available from the National Library of Australia

CONTENTS

WHAT IS DROUGHT?

In Australia, drought refers to the weather event that causes substantially lower than expected rainfall over a longer than expected period.

Drought occurs in natural cycles across Australia, and has long been a source of inspiration for poetry, songs, novels and folklore. The famous poem, My Country, published in 1908 and written by Dorothea Mackellar, refers to Australia's *"droughts and flooding rains"*.

Climate change now seems to be affecting the cyclic occurrence of droughts in Australia as warmer weather affects rainfall, evaporation and water supply. Warmer than normal temperatures can also contribute to the onset of a drought.

Deserts and semi-arid areas are not considered in drought, because low or no rainfall is expected in those regions.

Australia is the driest inhabited continent on Earth.

Antarctica is the driest continent since its fresh water is mostly frozen and not available for use by plants or animals.

DROUGHT DECLARED!

When a drought is officially declared by the Government of Australia, or by one of the States or Territories, the declaration becomes a trigger to make welfare and other assistance available to farmers who are under extreme drought-induced stress. A declaration of drought can also lead to the restriction of water use in cities, towns and on farms.

AUSTRALIAN BUREAU OF METEOROLOGY

The Australian Bureau of Meteorology produces drought statements that provide scientific advice to governments. These drought statements include statistics on rainfall, soil moisture, dam storage, flows in rivers, and the long-range weather forecast. The Bureau uses this information to predict the severity of a drought and advise the government, which can then officially declare the drought.

WHAT HAPPENS IN A DROUGHT?

FAILURE OF CROPS

Wheat crops need large amounts of water and are very vulnerable during droughts. Some Australian droughts have severely reduced wheat production and at times no wheat could be grown at all. Since wheat is a major Australian export, it provides significant income from overseas. When wheat is affected by drought, it affects the health of the whole Australian economy. Other non-native, water-hungry crops and exports such as cotton and rice are also greatly affected by drought.

DEATH OF LIVESTOCK

During a drought, rivers and dams can dry up. This can be disastrous for livestock farmers who may lose cattle and sheep that die from thirst. While some livestock may survive, they will be severely dehydrated and the quality of their meat and wool will be low. Some farms can use bore water, pumped from underground. However, not all bore water is drinkable and some of it is extremely salty.

DRY, CRACKED SOILS

After months or even years of no rain, farmland dries to dust and soil develops cracks. Winds blow the valuable topsoil away, leaving a hard surface behind. Semi-arid regions may become permanently arid following a prolonged drought.

ECONOMIC STRESS

Farmers can experience severe economic stress during a drought. With little or no income to pay utility bills or provide animals with food, they must make hard decisions about the suffering of their livestock. In cities and towns, shoppers notice higher food prices as farmers cannot provide enough produce to sell.

TOWN AND CITY WATER SUPPLIES

Town and city water reservoirs and dams can drop to dangerously low levels during a drought. Water may have to be supplied in water tankers to households. There will be water restrictions that prohibit the use of water for non-essential purposes, such as washing cars, hosing gardens or cleaning paths.

BUSH AND DROUGHT

Drought and flood cycles are natural in Australia. Many trees and plants have evolved with adaptations that enable them to survive with little water during droughts.

KANGAROOS

Kangaroos can stop producing joeys when there is a drought. Any joey embryo already in the female's body goes into a state of suspended growth called diapause, waiting until conditions are better for it to start to develop again. The dormant embryo will start to grow once the drought is over and there is plenty of food for the mother to eat. If a dehydrated kangaroo female cannot produce milk for her young during a drought, a joey in her pouch may die.

DROWNING IN MUD

As the water in rivers, creeks and dams evaporates, it leaves muddy areas that are traps for animals desperately seeking a drink. As they move further into the muddy pools to find water that is drinkable, they become caught in the sticky mud and may die there through drowning, exhaustion, or being attacked by animals that prey on them.

BUSH PLANTS AND TREES

Bush plant adaptations to drought have evolved over millions of years. Native plants have developed many ways to keep going, even when there is little or no rainfall.

GOLDEN WATTLE

These beautiful bushes with their masses of yellow flowers have narrow, waxy leaves that do not allow a lot of water to be lost by transpiration.

SCRIBBLY GUM

Scribbly gums develop a large bump just above the ground. This bump is called a lignotuber and it stores food and water. It can regenerate the tree if the top part dies during a drought or a bushfire.

GUMTREES

Gumtrees are iconic in Australia, growing everywhere from rainforests to open grassland. They have narrow, stiff leaves that do not dry out easily.

BOTTLE TREES

These unusual trees grow across the semi-arid areas of northern Australia. The trunk swells to an enormous size, storing food and water that the tree can draw on during very dry weather.

EMU BUSH

These plants have hairy, grey leaves. The colour reflects sunlight to keep the plant cool while the fuzzy covering provides insulation.

WHAT HAPPENS AFTER A DROUGHT?

When rain starts to fall again, rivers flow and dams fill. Although the falling rain provides relief for farmers, the effects are not immediate and life does not revert to normal overnight.

LIVESTOCK

A long drought in rural Australia may have forced some farmers to sell any livestock that was still alive. Restocking costs money and cannot be done until the parched land recovers enough to provide grass and other natural feed for the new livestock to eat.

AGRICULTURE

Dry fields may need a lot of rain before crops can be replanted. The land can be so dry that the first rain does little more than wet the surface layers. The degraded, hard soil will need fertilising and intensive care before it is ready to grow food again.

COUNTRY TOWNS

In some country towns, shops may need to close down during a severe drought, as local farmers give up and leave, or no longer have spare money to spend in town. The revival of these small towns can take years after a drought is over.

CITIES

In cities, people will slowly see food prices return to normal. They will start to water their gardens and hose their cars again once the local water authorities lift water use restrictions.

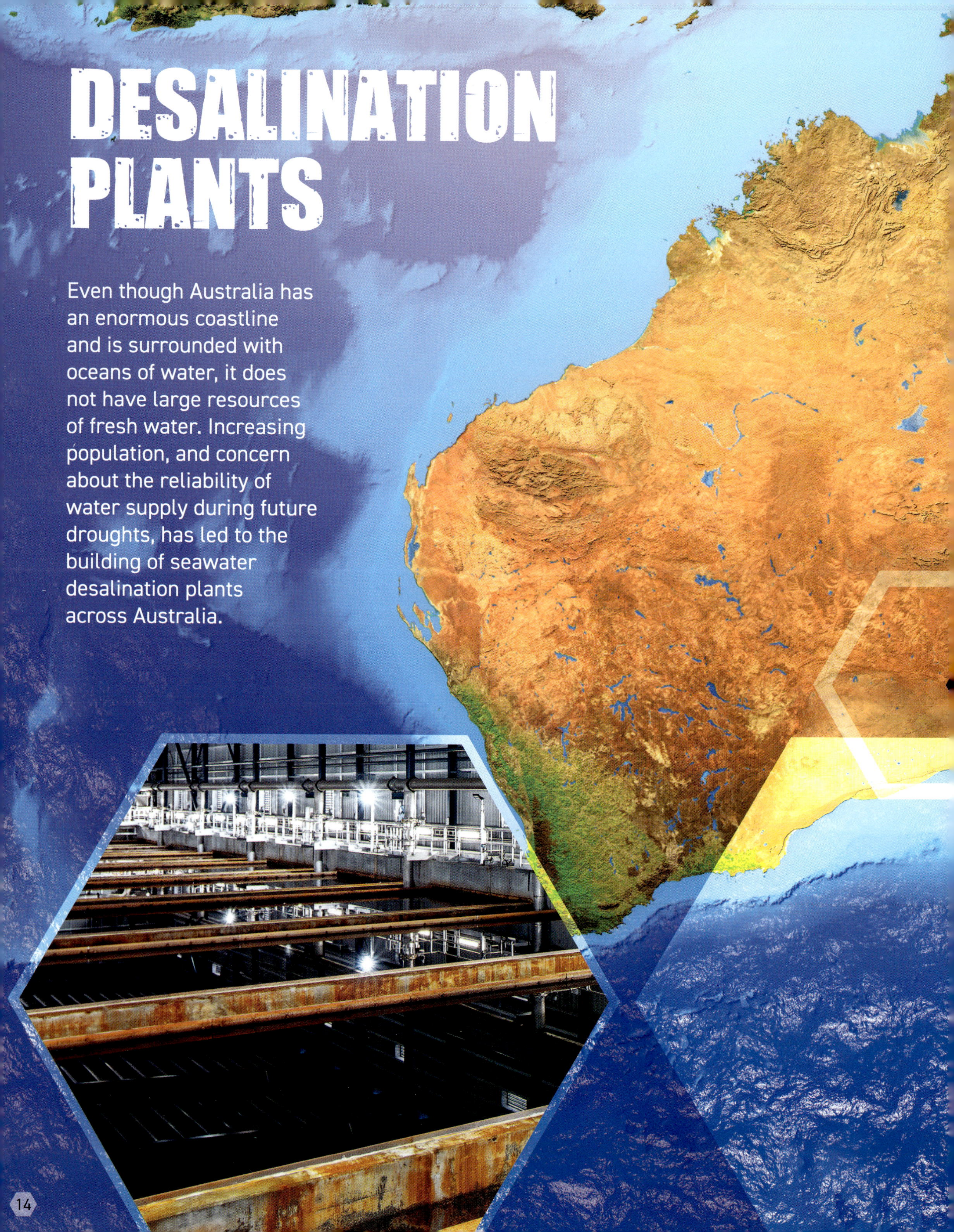

DESALINATION PLANTS

Even though Australia has an enormous coastline and is surrounded with oceans of water, it does not have large resources of fresh water. Increasing population, and concern about the reliability of water supply during future droughts, has led to the building of seawater desalination plants across Australia.

Desalination plants remove the salt from seawater and add the resulting fresh water into the public water supply. This process is costly and uses a lot of energy, but the security of the water supply for cities with millions of people is very important.

CLIMATE CHANGE AND DROUGHT

It is very likely that recent climate change and warming conditions across the planet have affected the frequency and length of the droughts experienced in Australia.

The severity of the 2017-2019 drought in Australia has been officially linked to the effect of climate change on weather conditions over Australia. Even Tasmania, a State which is usually well supplied with rain, became very dry. The shocking bushfires in the summer of 2019-2020 were a direct result of the drought conditions. This created an excess of dangerously dry vegetation in already fire-prone bushland.

EL NIÑO

El Niño is a Spanish term that means 'the boy'. It refers to a cyclic weather and oceanic event that occurs across the Pacific Ocean. Warm water during an El Niño phase can lead to drought across Australia. When the cycle changes to a cool water event, the phase is called La Niña, which means 'the girl' in Spanish. La Niña can be associated with heavy rains and flooding in Australia.

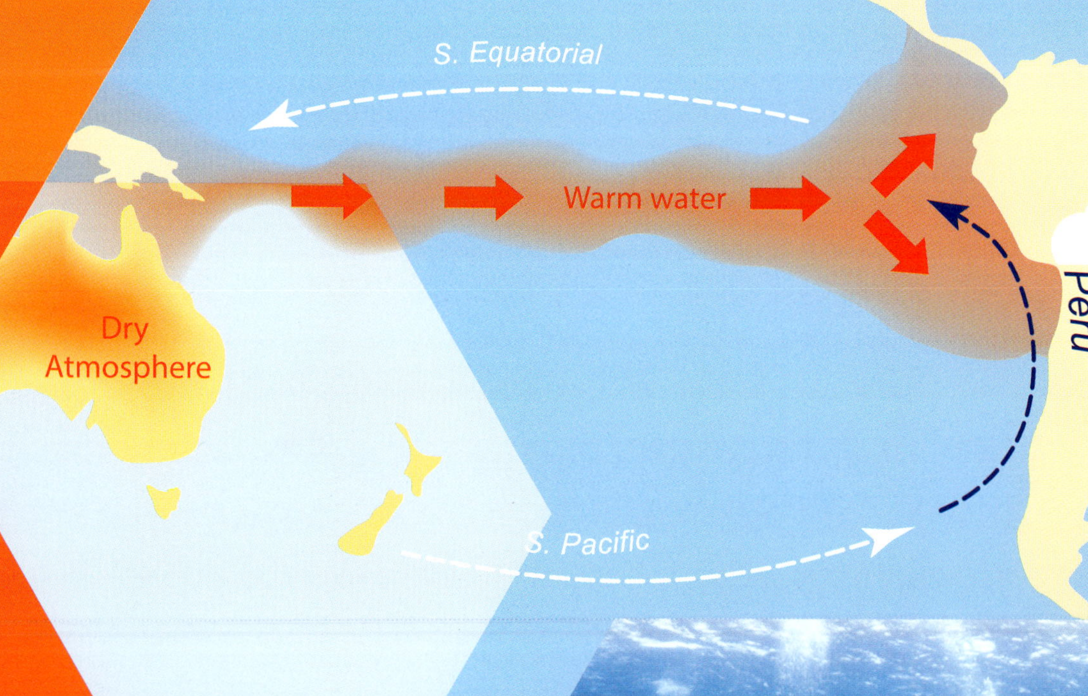

These two cycles have been occurring for thousands of years, but the Australian public has only used the names El Niño and La Niña over the last two decades.

Climate change seems to be affecting the timing and nature of the El Niño. Last century, the El Niño cycle occurred every few years, but in the last two decades El Niño seems to be happening more often. If an El Niño event occurs more frequently than in the past, we can also expect droughts to increase in frequency.

Frequent El Niño events can also cause unusual warming of the Pacific Ocean. This can lead to coral bleaching in the Great Barrier Reef.

DROUGHT AND BUSHFIRE

Hot, low-rainfall conditions during an El Niño-influenced drought will cause grassland and the bush to dry out and become prone to fire.

During a La Niña weather event, long periods of warm, wet conditions contribute to the increased growth of plants and trees. When an El Niño event follows La Niña, this excess of new vegetation will dry out too. This increases the amount of fuel that is available to burn and contributes to catastrophic bushfires. These cycles of drought and flood have been shaping Australian landscapes for millions of years.

FEDERATION DROUGHT 1895-1902

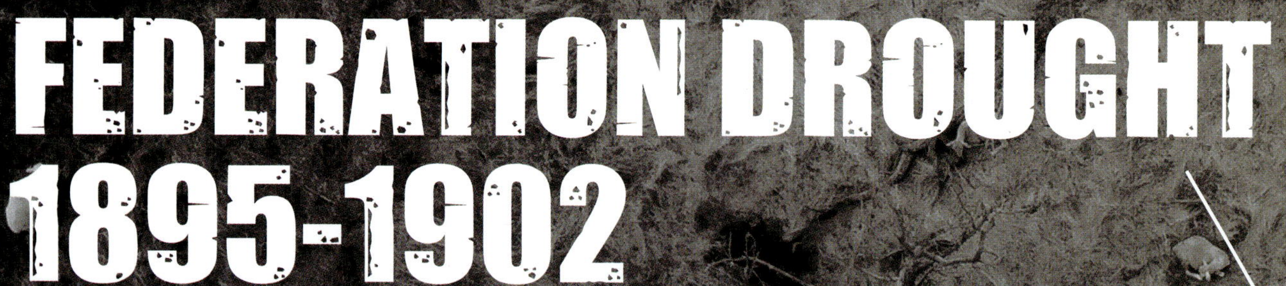

The long Federation Drought that occurred from 1895 to 1902 resulted in the deaths of over fifty million sheep. At that time, Australia depended on the high value of wool and the income from its export all around the world. The Federation Drought also killed millions of valuable cattle.

Before sealed roads were common, people frequently chose to travel on boats along rivers. This was a quicker and safer mode of transport than facing the uncertainty and discomfort of a lengthy cart ride along a bush track. However, during the long Federation Drought, rivers that were once fast-flowing turned into a series of waterholes. The Darling and Murray Rivers fell to such low levels that they were completely dry in some places. As a result, paddle steamers could no longer be used to transport people or farm produce.

WORLD WAR II DROUGHT 1937-1945

The dry weather across nearly all of Australia's food-growing regions during the Second World War added an extra burden onto people who were already suffering wartime food shortages.

Rg. D.1
No. V. B 990021
COMMONWEALTH OF AUSTRALIA
RATION BOOK
JUNE, 1943, ISSUE
Name
(BLOCK LETTERS)
Address
Civilian Identity No.
Or Alien Registration No.
SPECIMEN

On top of this, the dry weather led directly to the Victorian Black Friday bushfire of 1939. This was one of the worst bushfire events ever experienced in Australia. Many people died, as well as thousands of animals, and the economic impact was enormous.

At that time, Australia was heavily dependent on its sheep and wheat for prosperity and food. The World War II Drought had a disastrous effect on food production and the livelihoods of people around the country.

2017-2019 DROUGHT

Although this drought was shorter than others, its intensity was far greater. The winter rainfalls during the whole three-year period were unusually low. The drying effects of climate change, high temperatures and dry conditions even before 2017 all set the stage for a major drought.

When 2017 brought a severe lack of rain, the north of New South Wales and the Murray-Darling Basin were catastrophically affected.

The hottest average temperature ever recorded across Australia at the time was on 18 December 2019, at 41.88°C. The climax of these extreme conditions was the widespread bushfire emergency that occurred from the end of 2019 until the beginning of 2020.

SPECIAL REPORT

• THE MILLENNIUM DROUGHT 1997-2010 •

One of the worst periods of drought in Australia's recent history was the Millennium Drought, which lasted from 1997 until 2010. Many children grew up during this period never experiencing rain or knowing why an umbrella was needed.

FARMS AND BUSHLAND

Farmers endured the anxiety of having over a decade with no worthwhile rain, and watched their fields turn to dust. Crops either shrivelled up and died, or the soil was too dry to bother planting seeds at all. The dry topsoil blew away in the wind, making the farmland barren. When the drought finally broke, farmland needed fertilisers as well as water before it could start to grow crops again.

Without enough grass growing to feed livestock, farmers had to handfeed their animals or watch them die. The expense of having to buy feed for sheep and cattle led some farmers to give up and quit farming altogether.

CITIES AND TOWNS

Old, large trees started to lose their leaves, and lawns across the country browned and died. In Sydney, homeowners were told not to use water on their gardens. Instead, they were encouraged to save their shower or bath water and pour that onto their lawns and flowers. This had the unexpected advantage of turning some lawns greener than expected, since the phosphates in the soapy water acted as a fertiliser.

DAMS

At the time of the Millennium Drought, Sydney was Australia's biggest city by population. Its millions of people depended on water from Warragamba Dam, its main water source.

During the Millennium Drought, the water level in Warragamba Dam fell to a record level of only a third of the dam's capacity. Sydneysiders waited anxiously to see if imposed water restrictions were enough to maintain the supply. Would restrictions need to be extended, made more extreme, or would the water be turned off altogether? When substantial rain eventually fell, the drought was broken, and potentially dangerous restrictions were avoided.

ELECTRICITY

The Snowy Hydro is a hydroelectric power generating scheme. It uses pumped river water to turn turbines that generate electricity for southeastern Australia. Low river levels during the Millennium Drought affected this electricity supply.

• THE MILLENNIUM DROUGHT 1997-2010 •

HOME RAINWATER TANKS

Before the Millennium Drought, homeowners in cities were discouraged from using rainwater tanks, and in some areas the water from these tanks was considered unsafe to use because of contamination by metals, parasites and bacteria. Country and remote areas had been reliant on their own rainwater tanks since the beginning of non-Indigenous settlement.

The long Millennium Drought brought about a change in the attitude towards rainwater tanks in cities, and they are now a standard feature found in the yards of many homes. People can now choose whether to use rainwater or piped water for their household needs.

WATER RECYCLING

The need to recycle water in Australia's biggest cities turned into a major subject of discussion after the Millennium Drought.

Some new housing estates were developed with recycled water piping throughout, and several other recycling initiatives were introduced. These measures aim to make the growing populations of Australia's largest cities more drought-resilient and better able to survive the droughts that will occur in the future.

FUTURE DROUGHTS

There is no doubt that Australia will experience more droughts in the future. Climate change will probably make them more severe and of longer duration than in the past.

DROUGHT RESILIENCE

Being drought-resilient means having a plan of action to deal with future droughts. Governments, communities and individuals all have a role to play.

Drought-resilient measures will include:

- Building more water storage infrastructure and desalination plants
- Choosing drought-resistant crops and garden plants
- Water recycling
- Planning for looking after livestock
- Bushland management to reduce the risk of bushfires
- Farmland management to avoid loss of topsoil
- Avoiding polluting or degrading underground water

GLOSSARY

WORDS ABOUT DROUGHT

bore water underground water pumped to the surface

cyclic part of a cycle that regularly repeats

degraded of low quality

diapause when a kangaroo embryo pauses growth temporarily

dormant alive but in a suspended state

insulation substance that protects from temperature changes

lignotuber bump at the base of a tree for storing water and food

livelihood way of making an income to pay for things

parched very dry

regenerate bring back to life

revival improvement so that former conditions are restored

topsoil fertile soil on the surface of the ground

transpiration process plants use to raise water from the ground and out through their leaves

INDEX